COTTON GLOVES AND RUSTED ANCHORS

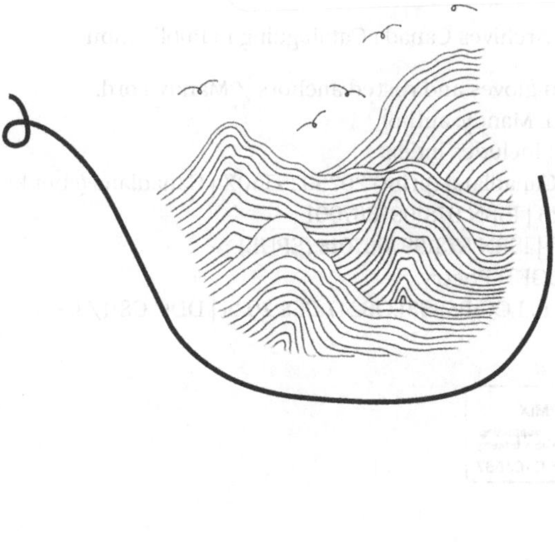

Mandy Ford

ISBN 978-1-997667-00-1

Series cover design by Vanessa Iddon of Perfect Day.
Design, layout, and editing by Brack and Brine.

Printed in Canada by Marquis Book Printing.
Published by Brack and Brine.

Inquiries regarding *Cotton Gloves and Rusted Anchors* may be directed to:

Brack and Brine
PO Box 1713 Stn B
Happy Valley-Goose Bay, NL
A0P 1E0 Canada

www.brackandbrine.com

Library and Archives Canada Cataloguing in Publication

Title: Cotton gloves and rusted anchors / Mandy Ford.
Names: Ford, Mandy, author.
Description: Includes index.
Identifiers: Canadiana (print) 2025025560X | Canadiana (ebook) 20250255626 | ISBN 9781997667001 (softcover) | ISBN 9781997667018 (EPUB)
Subjects: LCGFT: Poetry.
Classification: LCC PS8631.O6247 C68 2025 | DDC C811/.6—dc23

MIX
Paper | Supporting responsible forestry
FSC® C103567
FSC www.fsc.org

This book is for the self that navigated rough seas, for the heart that kept beating through the weight of it all, and for the soul that still found beauty in the darkness. Dedicated to the versions of me who never gave up. To the silent battles, the sleepless nights, the thoughts that screamed you can't, and the courage that whispered, watch me.

contents

513

home is still there

the levee

they build the dam or don't
we're damned anyway
our confidence like the spring in May

(melting)

this back and forth
the rising tides above our heads
how can you rest in your bed?

(peacefully)

tell me there's no mercury
tell me there's nothing to see
a history of chances
giving away what isn't ours
we criticize the scarred earth
wonder why there's not enough ice

there's no choice
our words float out with the tide
riding on the waves of all we seem to have forgotten
all we've never learned from
drifting toward the levee that we're still paying for

pop's wharf

walking along the shore a little past noon
eight pieces of sea glass in my pocket
(blue the most valuable)
i had on sandals with no socks

aunt warned me about rubber boots
  and mice spilling in over the side
down at my toes
so i figured
why wear rubbers?

my naked toes exposed
i was careful for the seaweed
  and the sea lice surely tangled in it
i watched for beach spiders
  that could haunt my bed at night
avoided being "too involved" with the grass

an armful of driftwood under my left
and a leash in my right hand
not that i ever needed it
the dog galloped and swallowed salt water
like he'd never seen dry land

pop's stage in the distance
i'd sit for half a day
catching sculpins with twine and bent nails
(it can be done)
even flatfish if you're good enough

the sun sneaks in through the clapboard
and paints who i was before
a tiny picture
just enough to remember
that home is still there
and memories won't fade
unless you let them

twine

this family was knit with twine
laced with careful time-worn fingers
prepared as a duty
patterned by past confessions
the holes sewn feverishly

should we get lost in the storm
no one can say
we didn't try our best
no one can say
our net wasn't cast long or hard enough

we sit idly in this ship
comparing ourselves to others
as we go down without words
pretending as a duty
that the twine was enough

variables

strung out
(sprung out)
on the white picket fence
babbling blue target jays
snowbirds in their own right
whisper down to the edges of all that was forgotten
“you'll end up your mother”

pale daisies kissed by sunlight
we might go on dancing
without movement
our swelling minds
lost in the afterwards
when we break
when we shake
hands after supper
and dishes become reasons
to forget and not forgive

roots

you didn't dig my roots
you didn't even burrow

but everyone loves a sturdy evergreen
in the right light
thrown in the middle of barren land

my advice to you
is not to sell seeds
you never plan to sow

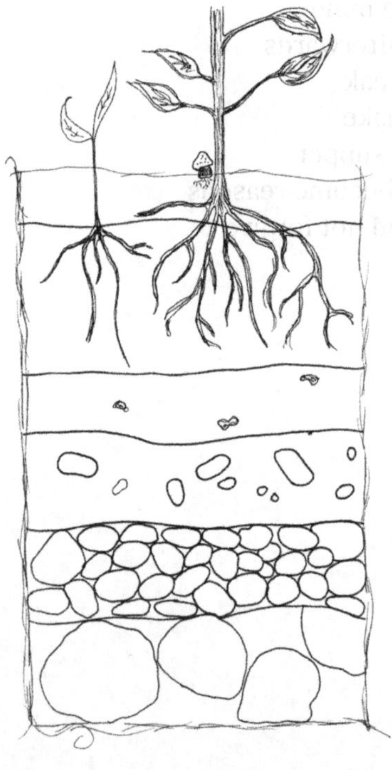

it's only a minute

there is something to be said
for saying something
when nothing
no one
comes together
cares

looking from warm windows
still or embracing
supper cooking
children's faces clean
I want for you
all of the things i cannot give
  names on their mittens
  awards on the shelf

it's only a minute
before the memory is made
a moment wrapped in silver and gold
"it's exactly what i wanted!"

it's only a minute
before the memory is gone
no one looking from the windows
no one warming their bones

running
and walking
and standing
are very different things

small harbour

colour me atavistic

i can fit here beside
these bottles
these knives

open up your lonely eyes

we will not be pardoned by sunlight
but by the valley
of sea-salted bones
of those who came before
who knew the way of kindness
of necessity

you drew them out
and bled them dry

now whitewashed houses
and well-worn shoes
sit collecting dust
in this harbour

wrestling the changing tides
with cotton gloves
and rusted anchors

the TLH in april

i found the draft
and caught the chill
between my fingers

time passes quicker than lights

we all stop and watch a youngster
cross the road
holding our breath
hoping everyone's obeying the rules

this road is *long*
and *soggy*

it's the TLH in April
when you're never quite sure
you've got the clearance needed
and you pray to God or Moses
someone comes to get you
if you're more than eight hours on the road

i found the draft
and caught a chill

rolling up the window
i ended the airstream
connecting me to the Mealies
and all the trees supporting my habit
of cold deep breathing

crow songs

crows converse behind my house
beating their wings against the orange sky

puff of breath
rustle of twigs

they tell the truth
they joke
they sing

radio silence

you don't feel the night like i do

silk between my fingers
home without the walls
i can be here with this empty space
beside me
inside me

i am not afraid
in the black

i fight back

never alone
in the radio silence

could have been Anthony

my jaw clicks
the same as my uncle's
and my dad's
i often wondered
had i been born with
or without a purpose
had i been an Anthony
instead of what i am
would i be any different?

would i be
a parent
a poet
a-fraid?

i have built engines
i have cut trees
i have fought wars eternal
i have kissed a girl
i have raised my voice
i have fallen in defeat
spent
and i am just as lost as ever

my jaw clicks
but only when i'm trying to tell you
that it doesn't matter

<- you

don't love me back

sixty percent

maybe we drown
maybe we live
our lives are always underwater

every envelope is meant to be
pushed
punished

you're wearing your green dress now
inviting me in
keeping me safe
swallowing me whole

it's after three and i can see
this is the beginning
of the end
of broken heart syndrome

maybe we drown
maybe we live
walking around sixty percent water

same eyes

i once asked a boy to marry me
and he looked at me like i had more heads
than a bucket of nails

by marry i meant love
by love i meant "could stand to be around"
in silence
tightly holding hands
wishing and hoping
looking at the moon

i once asked a girl to marry me
and she looked at me like i had more heads
than a bucket of nails

by marry i meant love
by love i meant "could stand to be around"
in silence
tightly holding hands
wishing and hoping
looking at the stars

there's really no difference
we're all one and the same
beneath the same dark sky
wanting for nothing but the chance
to view those stars
and that moon
with the same eyes

every night

maybe i do
go to the valley of the shadow of us
every night

i smell that woodsmoke
i see that constellation
i am alone between
where you and i were
and whatever's next

it's safe to say
there's nobody like you
it's safe to say
i broke my own heart too

every night
i burn away the memories
i block out the sky
i am alone in the
in-between
where you and I
were you and I

exodus

bursts of birds billow
against the sharp winter sun
and i navigate fields of coarse blonde hair
lost

frost shatters all corners
life moves slowly
and with purpose
a lover's hand its equal

we meander through these feelings
testing the weight of our tongues
against the truth

inside the sandstorm

trying to keep an open mind
or at least a clear one
i see you everywhere

it's like a curse that follows
until we're not busy
then it comes creeping
with the power to make me lose
water from my eyes

aches in my bones
like a mental arthritis
you just keep calling
with all those dark treetops
and faded sunsets
and frogs singing
and boats boating
and lazy Sundays licking ice cream
and buying useless lawn chairs

it always comes creeping
just when i start to forget
i'm still inside the sandstorm
with or without you

new moon

when you fell into my sky
it was purple and orange
it was blessed with yellow flowers and honey bees
there was no need to command attention
when you fell out of my sky
it was dark, sheer, and damp with regret

i write about the way
your skin was warm velvet
your hair left its scent on all my pillows

i buy the yellow flowers
i tell the bees to go back home
i look away from the moon
when it commands my attention

there's not a minute i don't miss
the hope you gave me
that love was real
and i was capable

i'm going out on
all of the smallest limbs here
assuming your love

i always say we
when it was i
to include you
in all the spaces
where you
left
yourself
out

you and i may not rhyme
but we are my favorite words

i blossom for you
against my better judgement

hope everlasting

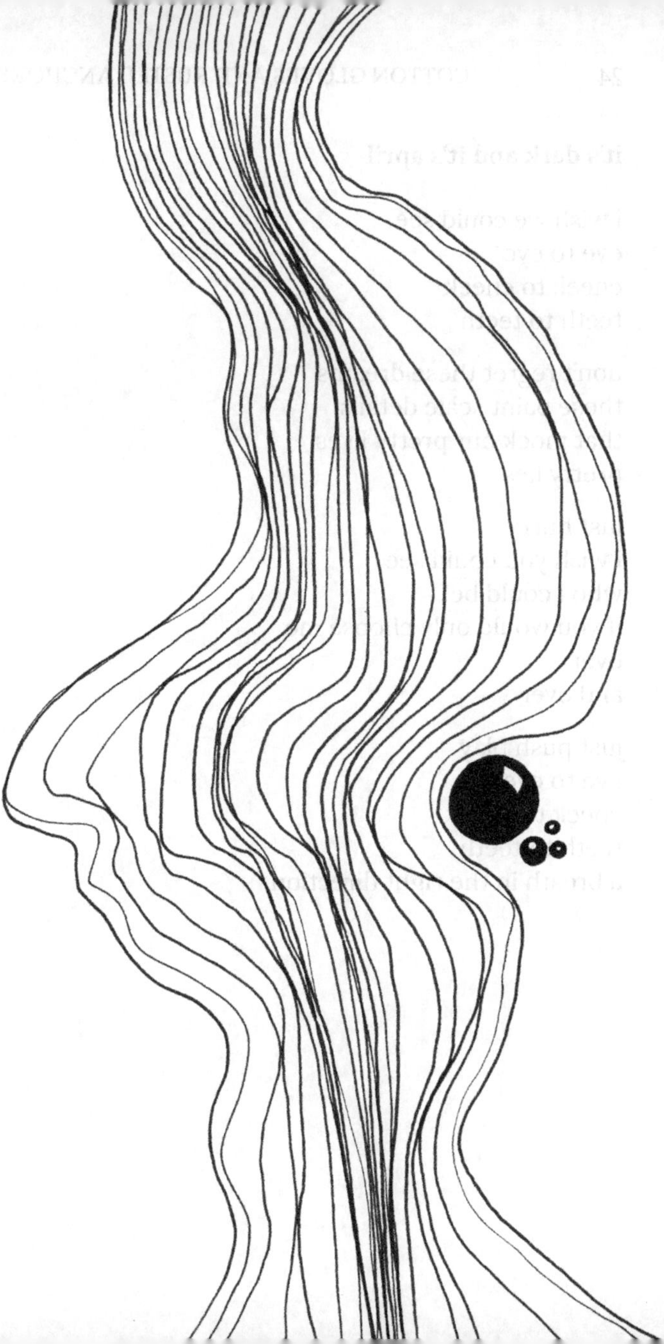

it's dark and it's april

i wish we could see
eye to eye
cheek to cheek
teeth to teeth

don't regret these dreams
these paint scale details
that mock our pretty lives
pretty lies

just hurry
i wish you could see
who i could be
if you would only choose me
over
and over

just push play
eye to eye
cheek to cheek
teeth to teeth
a breath in the right direction

untouchable

you're always in that spot
sweetly
untouchable
nestled in the back of my mind
where rhymes are made
and plans are laid
and best-kept secrets stain the halls

a simple touch
our values fold
our hearts grow old

you're always in that spot
with parted lips
and steady hips
why can't we find a quiet place?
a warm embrace?
the best-kept secrets hide in the walls

why must you be so
untouchable?

mismanagement

i think of you
as if no time has passed
no leaves have fallen
nor snow
since that day

that moment my heart cracked into three pieces
one for you
one for me
and one for the life that would never exist

i hear that crack in every song
feel it in every breeze
taste it like copper thrown into corners
 and forgotten
wait for it every second

somehow you've managed
 to make me invisible to myself
i look in the mirror and i don't know what i see
just shapes
lines
curves
hardened eyes

today i held a piece of the earth in my hands
and poured myself out in droplets

they say your whole life flashes before your eyes
 when you die

i hope you're excluded

woman of letters

katsek

there's a natural cadence to it
the exact width of my patience

i pencil you in indefinitely

let's not make a racket

it is always autumn in my heart
no matter what set of eyes meet mine

we are different kinds of broken
none of us whole
(strength in numbers)

someday i may tell you
that you are all of my Novembers
and that every November ends up breaking me
shaking down my soul
and eating me alive

i hold myself together
writing free-verse poems
that don't even feel free

small hands

i look at these small hands
brilliant hands
hands i thought were big
until i compared
put them up against the big black sky
forgetting why
i was here

these small hands
write their way off the page
bleeding rage
and sometimes flowers

let's find common ground
inside this black inkwell
with our small hands
holding fast
forgetting why

my life on these shelves

my life on these shelves
astronomy
french-english dictionary
photography
i tried to be the person i was before
but the pain wasn't worth it
that's not who i am anymore
i'm still figuring this out

my life on these shelves
biographies
Black Ink
Woman of Labrador (i think)
i tried to be the person you deserved
but the pain wasn't worth it
you're not who you were anymore
i wish i had figured this out earlier

my life on these shelves
i'm still dipping in this ink well

address

it all ends up in the landwash
out with the tide
in with the times
over there with your emotions
bent at the knees
begging for direction
we're ironclad with our devotion
not as black and white as wrong or right
i just write

i just wanted to be a woman of letters
but the problem is
i've forgotten your address

a book

sometimes a book can tell you how to live
how to paint your house
and wear your hair
how to keep a man and bed him best
and provoke a religion inside your watery edges

a book can be a powerful thing
a bomb of phrases and slithery truths
a sleuth
a saviour with silky pages
the closest you'll ever get to Athens
the farthest you'll go from home

sometimes a book can tell you how to live
or just tell you that you are not

unravel

just knowing you is like
trying to breathe under water

you fill my lungs with choked up memories
my ears with whispers
and my heart with uncertainty

i try to swim up to the surface
reaching desperately for a hand that isn't there

your heart is somewhere else
beating warm underneath the covers
of another's bed

i fear that this will end come morning
that i'll be back to confronting demons alone
there are books full of words
that vouch for my existence
but you read none of them

buttons and zippers

you occupy a notable place
beneath my ribs
underneath will and reason

you found your way
despite the thorns and shattered glass
despite resistance and doubt

i occupy a notable place
beneath your hands
stinging with lust and patience

i found my way
despite the buttons and zippers
keeping us apart

we occupy a notable place
on Johnson Hill Road
beneath the oak tree
on your old brown blanket
feeling things that lack forgiveness

anatomy of ink

strange concepts
parallel hearts
not necessarily in love
but knitted with purpose

these streets and buildings turn us inside out
put rot in our heads

we are solid in our bones and in our ways
sinking beneath the fold
and separating at atlas C1
trying to conceal our humanity
with vanity

do not forget how it's done
(living)

you can borrow my pen if you need to understand
the anatomy of ink

anew

there's nothing about something
i loved always
you were the lucky one
walking away
avoiding the scar
you're still here
coherent and thriving

i'm picking up the words you left
forming new sentences
never missing a beat
finding a life that is worth the defeat
sailing down the hill
in a dory made of wishes
a signal without the flare
trying so hard
writing myself anew

with

i need a writer
a poet
someone who understands
matters of the soul
someone to grow old with
raise a child with
make a home with
cook dinner with
grow a garden with
bike with
make music with
buy drapes with
mark anniversaries with
celebrate life with
share sorrows with
fuck
tell stories to
and embark on adventures with
if you know this poet
tell him where to find me

seriousness of condition

when i saw it i think my heart stopped beating
for a second
my face was warm
heart rattled
i saw a ghost

these treasures are no comparison
to a warm body
to a friendly smile
i saw a ghost

is it easy for you?
we're all speaking with borrowed words
but you can't plagiarize my mind

stuck in this salty aquarium
i swear i'm not a clockwise pessimist
holding a glass over the flame

i'm burnt out
i should be done by now
you'd think i'd be done by now
seeing all these ghosts of Christmas past

you should get this one framed
i should run away

i'm some kind of monster

shoreless

i stared at the word
until it made no sense to me
just a grey blur on the page
am i making the same mistake twice?
i didn't understand poetry at first

i wish i could trust people's predictions
the uncertainty eats me up
vitally i'm twenty beats ahead
visually a dozen behind
what's left?
not enough change in my range

stumbling through my sentence
I stared at the world
until it made no sense to me
just a blur across the stage

what if i couldn't tell you my stories
i'm just a civilian
not quite a lady
with lace ambitions

lick the ground

changing lanes

i am living on the ground
falling down from being up
and getting up from falling down
confined within these measurements

bare birch tree see me
lying beneath your branches
waiting for answers

quiet

the kind of quiet you can't understand
without closed eyes
and weightless hands

no security in
intertwinement
just the echo of a heartbeat
before your decision

a tender idea
without closed eyes

we see a world more perfect than
tiny hands can grasp and i
find comfort in the intertwine
the days that i
knew the quiet

practice

"practice being normal"
i make no sound
lying in silence
the world is not real, really
listen for a whisper
drip
tick-tock
drip

"practice being extraordinary"
i make all the sounds
bells and whistles
chapstick and flats
lipstick and heels
baby we are still young
we look like ourselves
just like everyone else
in danger of being on fire
we melt inside our clothes

"practice being normal"
numb
surreal

lick the ground

i need to live on earth again
to touch the soil instead of the keyboard
i need to feel the wind again
to feel life instead of stale familiarity

i count my blessings
the plants in my window
i consider them to be five
as long as the lights are turned off

we are so afraid of living
of touching
apologizing for advances
that would have once gained a smile

we are so afraid of living
of dying
of breathing
the germs on my table won't kill me today

i could lick the ground
if everyone would believe me

weight

i can feel my heart pounding in my ears
it's not fear
it's just the weight
(just)
that i carry around
three times the average gravitational pull

i am quick
i am fluent
but i am heavy
it is a burden
shared by my relations
(they like to remind me)
that someone prettier
skinnier
has it all
some words stick to me like tape
(even if only said once)
and i struggle to peel them off
to not repurpose the tape for their mouths

i am quick
i am fluent
but i am heavy
the weight of your resistance
is more than my legs can carry

forget
release

meet me at my watery edges
cast your judgements aside
and find that you are free
there are no eyes on you but mine
forget
release
accept fate and all of its disclaimers
the distance between you and your desires
is a fleeting thought
amid the rot of your doubt
forget
release
cast your judgements aside
and breathe your deepest breath
the only thing holding you back
is you

think of me like a house

think of me like a house
with a hundred compact rooms
filled with antiques and broken mirrors
the bones are still good

think of me like a house
with mismatched chairs
and vaulted ceilings
my height is my advantage

think of me like a house
where you hold your love for safekeeping
where your secrets stay within the walls
i peel them off like wallpaper

think of me like a home
where we are safe
and gloriously free

the feeling and the noise

between the feeling and the noise
i've found all but simple pleasures
trickling down to a puddle of bedlam
we wet our feet in yesterday's mistakes
making promises for a better tomorrow
it's a shame we're all bad liars

whose face

i don't know whose face
to picture in the midnight hours
between thinking and sleeping
longing and breathing
when the moment holds its own eclipse
we're passing through
just thoughts nailed to a door
that never gets shut
i don't know whose face
just like i don't know my own
i lay awake burning
the bridge as it gets built
longing and breathing
until sleep says hello

life ablaze

clouds ablaze
soft tissue
pink and scarred
floating
reminding me that life is
bigger
broader
more settled with time

moving mountains
and burning bridges
are all a part of the movement
that plays pretend
while we break and bend
doing our best to make amends

pink tissue in the sky
life ablaze in July

late english rose

her words are soft pink
petals of a late english rose
she sees herself in the backdrop
  of every 80s teen movie
her hair flows orange against the fading sun

she looks at me like i have all the answers
the yellow warblers on her dress
match the quirks of her smile
she's everything you'd want to be
if you were a girl's girl

I look in the mirror and i find no trace of her
just lines of faded mascara
and premature frowns
but she stands behind me
and that is enough

happy hour

happy minute
happy second
it doesn't seem to last long
when you open your mouth and failure falls out
i wish i could blame it on something or someone
but it's always been me
and my inability to see

happy minute
happy second
the times you hold closest to your vital organs
the times that seem shorter than their allowances
the times that slip away so easily

things we found in silence

there are some things we keep secret
moving lightly
treading water
whispering

the night knows your story
even if no one else ever will
it knows how you looked with your back to the field
accepting an embrace not given with love
it knows how lost your eyes were
how hollow your heart felt remembering

there are some things we keep secret
even when we want to scream
to jump
to sink
we just fade into the background noise
lost in moments that have gathered age
whispering the things we found in silence

skin

i decorate my skin with signs
that I've felt something
done things in my life
made memories
had dreams and desires

i decorate my skin in black ink
stark contrast
to my sensitive white
yet native body

i decorate my skin with modern fragrances
to wash away all the scents
that say i am normal and womanly
without need for covering

i decorate my skin with cotton and denim
to hide my perfectly
imperfect form
from steel glances

you decorate my skin with your lips
i find that's the best cover up
for a life that needs no hiding

upended

One thing I have noticed, since i began wringing my fists, is my knuckles. For whatever reason, they're more prominent on my left hand, even though that's not my dominant hand. There are things I have been noticing since I started losing weight that no one else but me would notice. Because I'm the only one in this vessel. There is a suffocating weight on my chest. Displaced from everywhere else, perhaps?

Everyone loves to put on a pink shirt and clap their hands for Bell Let's Talk, but I'm not sure how many actually mean it when they ask, “How are you?” I don't think they really want to know, because it would make them far too uncomfortable.

I used to write whenever something stirred an emotion in me. And now I wait. I wait it out in silence. Because who knows who is reading this? What conclusions they must draw, sitting in their own wooden boxes waiting for the light?

I read a quote recently that said moths were more beautiful than butterflies because they always find the light (in every situation). It is not lost on me that I always turn off the light when I see them coming.

index

titles

first lines

Best Wishes

About the Author

Mandy Ford is a lifestyle blogger and artist raised in Fox Harbour, NunatuKavut. Having lived in Happy Valley-Goose Bay since 2012, she spends her free time writing, exploring and photographing the landscapes and curiosities of life in Labrador. When she is not working to preserve cultural heritage in southern Labrador, you're likely to find her off-roading with her husband Jeffrey and dog Kane.

Brack and Brine publishes beautiful books that matter to the North.

SEPARATION POINT

Michael Friis Johansen

a Labrador crime thriller

(fiction, forthcoming 2025)

NURSE FORTESCUE & DOCTOR PADDON

Dave Paddon

true stories of wartime medicine and frontier healthcare

IN THE SHADOW OF TUNGUSUAK

Chris Buckley

a true story of two brothers and adventure in the Torngat Mountains

2025 Foreword INDIES Silver Winner

AND YOU CAN'T HELP BUT LISTEN

Jamie Jackman

the poems and lyrics of Labrador's award-winning Silver Wolf Band

"profoundly stunning lyrics"
—Maggie McLean, *The East*

Labrador, a reader's guide

Robin McGrath

reviews and essays on Labrador books

"McGrath's personal story gives this book a spine."

—Joan Sullivan, *The Telegram* (St. John's)

LABRADOR CINEMA

Mark David Turner
& Morgen Mills

a visual history of 120 years of Labrador film

2024 IPPY Awards Silver Medal

---

brackandbrine.com